Ugly
Holiday Sweaters
COLORING BOOK

Ellen Christiansen Kraft

Dover Publications, Inc.
Mineola, New York

Nothing says "holiday spirit" like an ugly sweater! This coloring collection contains the worst of the worst— the sweaters feature reindeer, angels, fruitcakes, and more obnoxious designs perfect for family photos. The latest edition to Dover's *Creative Haven* series for the experienced colorist, the detailed illustrations are perfect for experimentation with media and color technique. Plus, the perforated pages make displaying your work easy.

Bibliographical Note

Ugly Holiday Sweaters Coloring Book is a new work, first published by Dover Publications, Inc., in 2015.

International Standard Book Number

ISBN-13: 978-0-486-80377-7
ISBN-10: 0-486-80377-5

Manufactured in the United States by RR Donnelley
80377505   2015
www.doverpublications.com

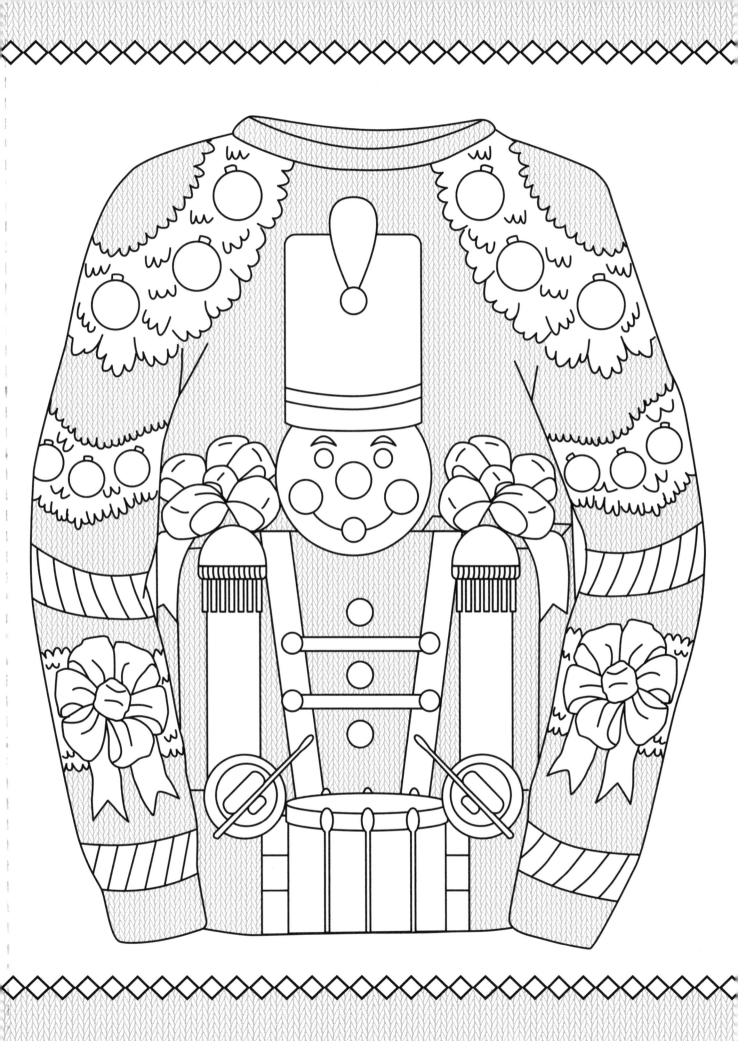

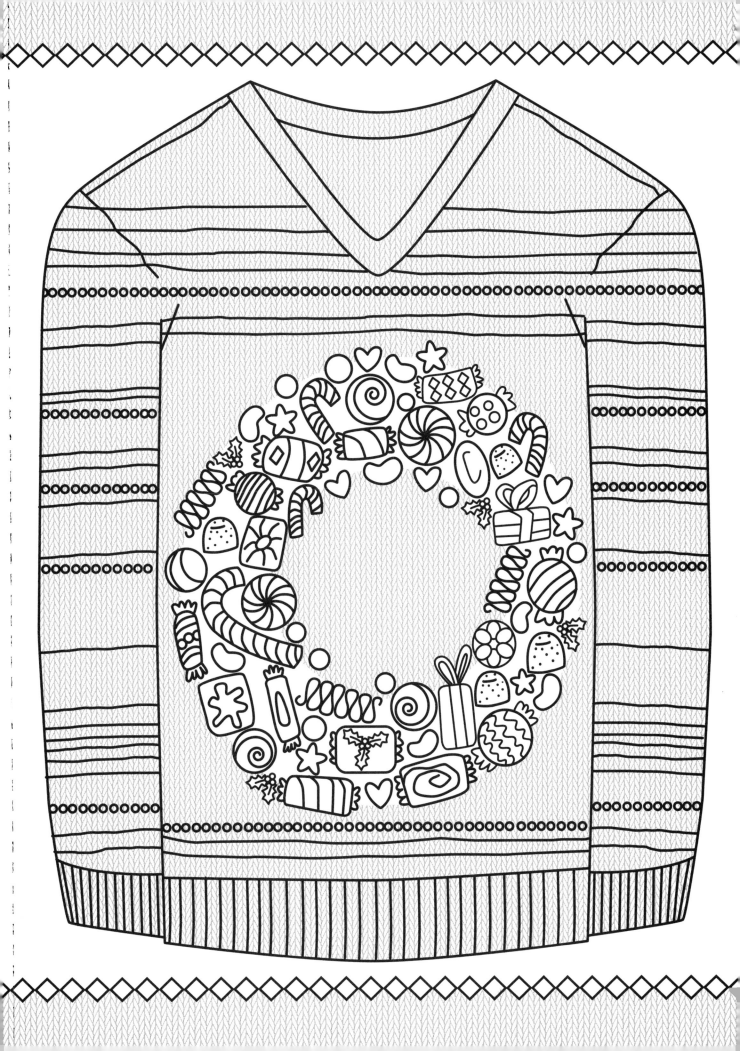

A Partridge in a Pear Tree

Two Turtle Doves

Three French Hens

Four Calling Birds

Five Golden Rings

Six Geese a-Laying

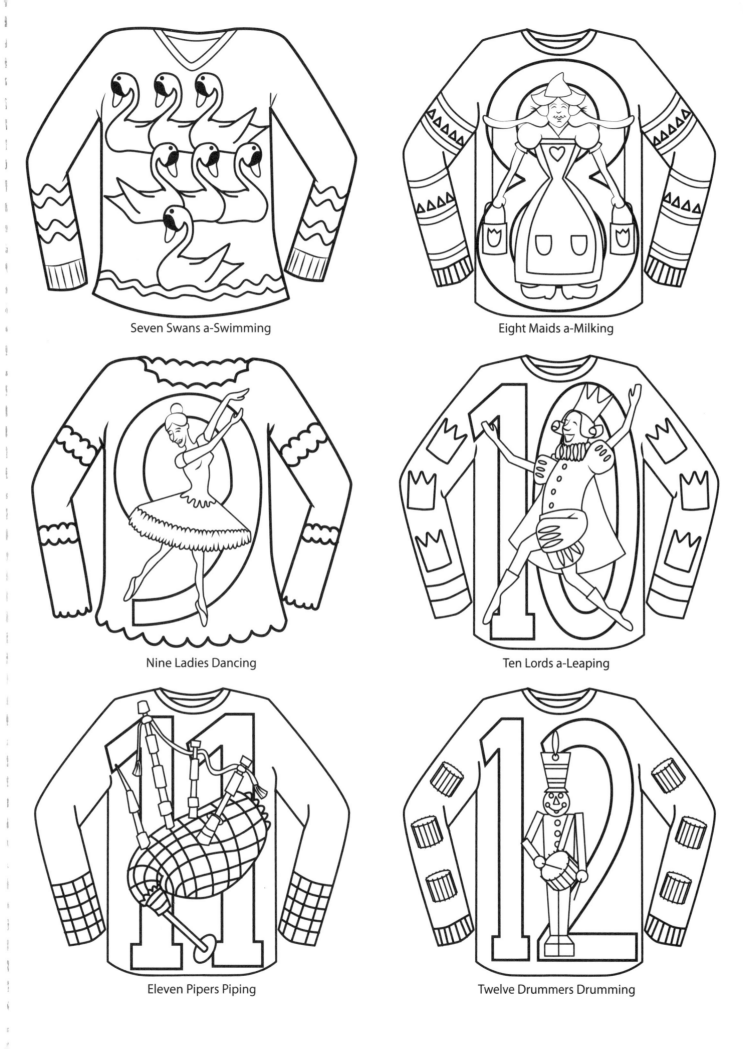

Seven Swans a-Swimming

Eight Maids a-Milking

Nine Ladies Dancing

Ten Lords a-Leaping

Eleven Pipers Piping

Twelve Drummers Drumming

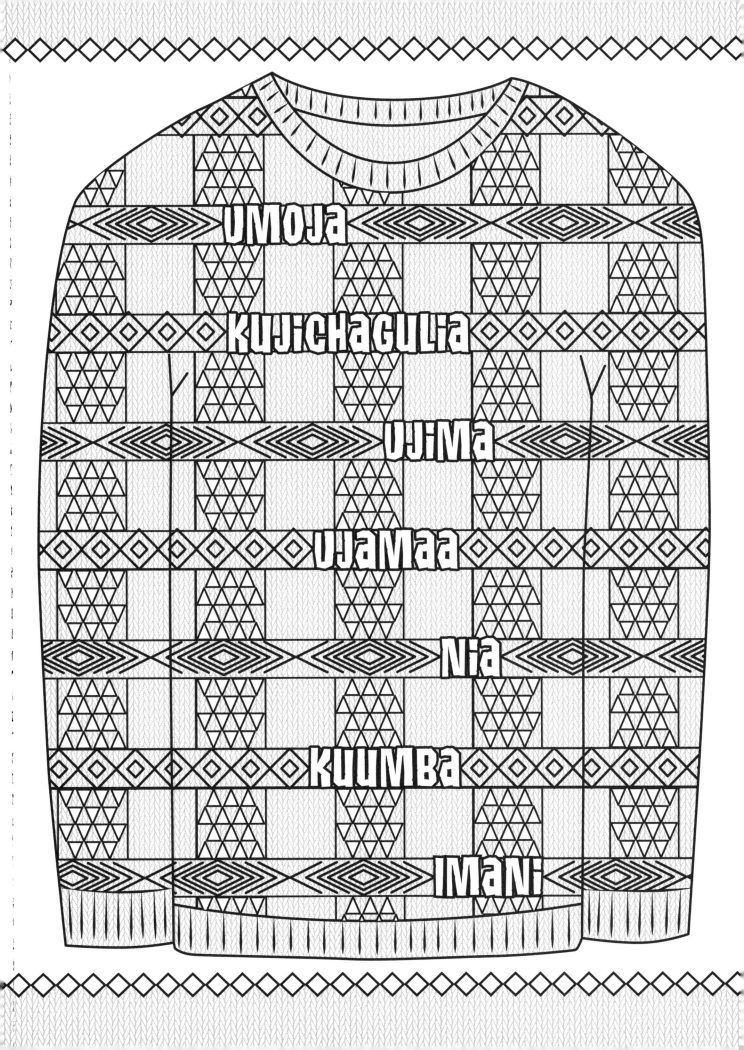

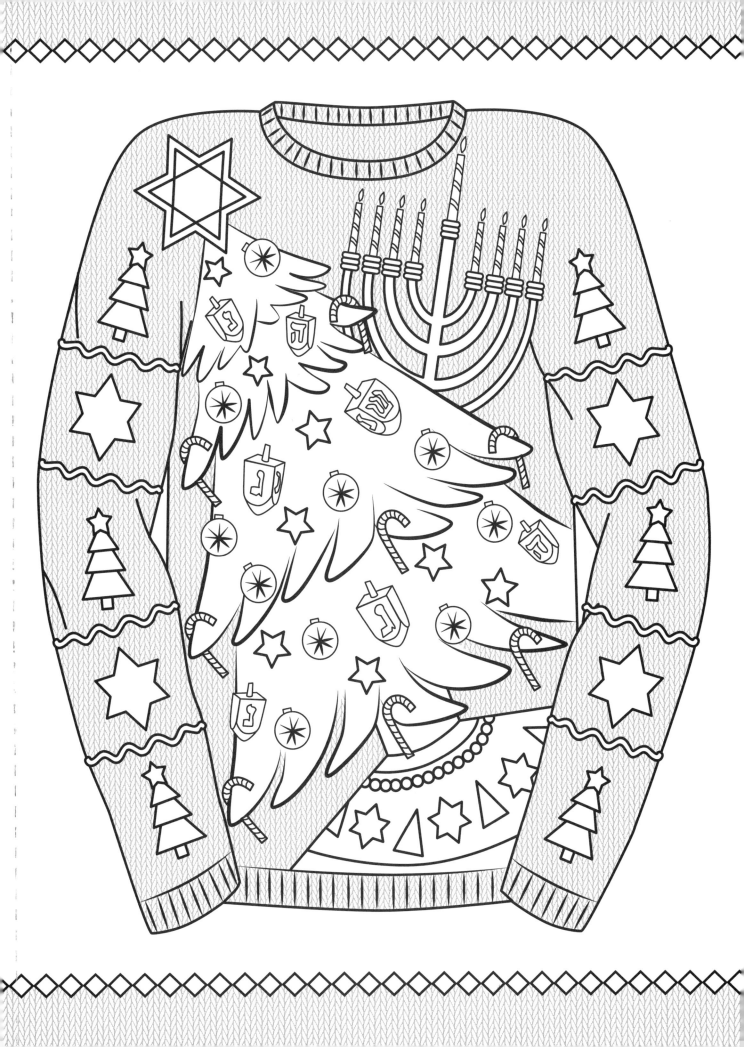

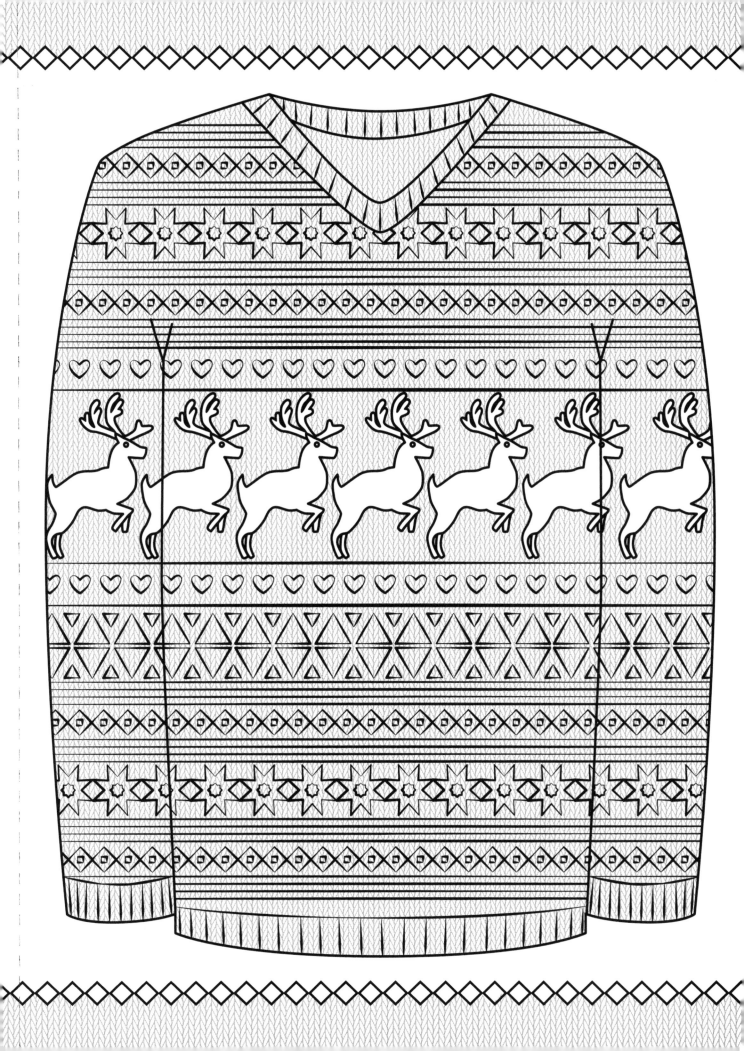

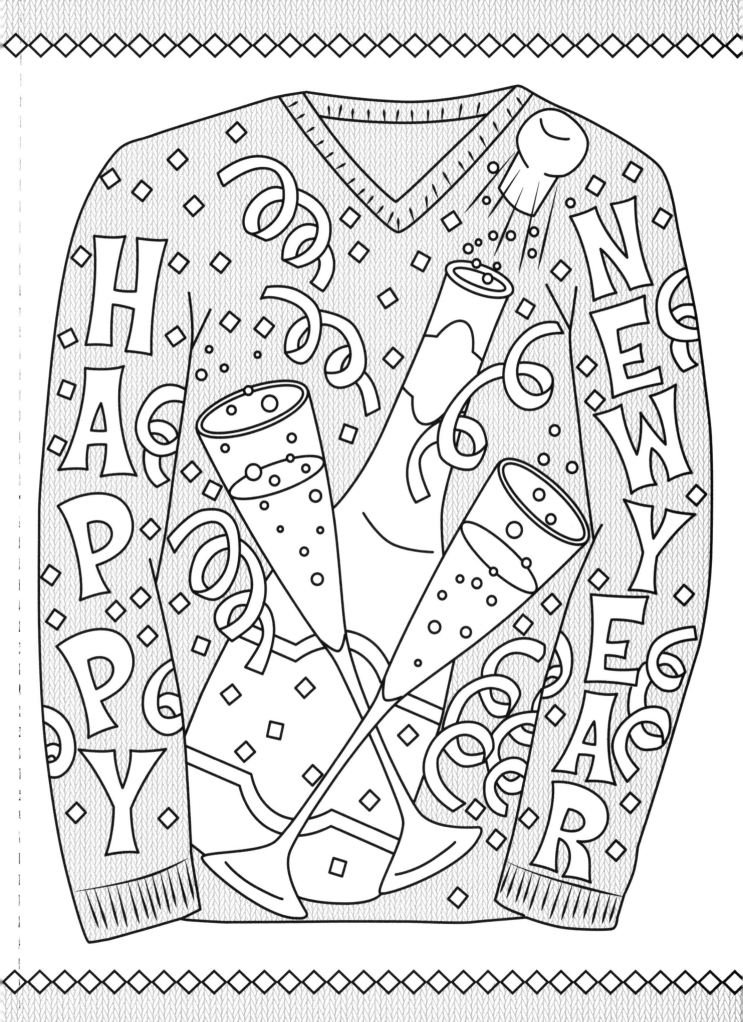